Jesus

Still in the Business of turning Water into Wine!!

by Mike Shatto

RoseDog✿Books

PITTSBURGH, PENNSYLVANIA 15238

RoseDog Books
585 Alpha Drive, Suite 103
Pittsburgh, PA 15238
Visit our website at *www.rosedogbookstore.com*

ISBN: 978-1-4809-8227-7
eISBN: 978-1-4809-8204-8

I've often pondered what it would be like to write a book about my life. I've never seen myself as being any kind of writer—just an ordinary guy—but it was something I always thought about. My life has certainly been a journey with much of the same struggles many other people go through and live with. However, today, knowing Jesus as my Lord and Savior and seeing how God's unending grace has played out in my life is what gave me the motivation and purpose to actually do it. It all began July 11, 1961, when I came into this world. I already had a checkmark against me as my mother, still a kid herself, was only sixteen years old. She did marry my father, who was also a teenager, but it did not last and ended in divorce probably before my second birthday. He chose to never be a part of my life, which was difficult and damaging for me to understand as a child, and more so as an adult. The details of my life as a baby and toddler remain a secret, which is probably for the best. My earliest memories begin when I lived at my grandmother's house with my mother. Soon after my fifth birthday, my mother chose to move in with her boyfriend, who was very abusive.

Little did I know, a lifelong nightmare was about to begin for me. It was after the move, I remember, that the sexual abuse started by some kids in the neighborhood. I had no idea or understanding of what was happening.

The physical and mental abuse toward me from my mother's boyfriend was horrible. He treated me like a piece of trash, telling me how worthless I was and always would be. I just could not understand his anger and hate for me, and yet, my mother witnessed it every day and did nothing. She always allowed it to go on. She would never say a word against him or in my defense when he would mistreat me. There was no such thing as love in this place I was forced to live in. My mother never married this man, but she went on to have three children with him. He did not abuse them as harshly as he did me. I vividly remember one Christmas, each of my siblings got a bicycle, but there wasn't one for me. I dared not even ask where mine was. I can still feel the disappointment of that day.

A regular occurrence for me was getting beat with a paddle or a belt by him. It happened very often and for the littlest thing I did wrong. The worst beating I still recall to this day was with a hose when I was around seven years old. I have no recollection of what I had done to deserve such a punishment, but I remember getting beaten over and over with that hose so badly that I actually stopped crying because I had no more tears left. I just wanted to get through it and gritted my teeth waiting for him to finally stop hitting me. It was like he enjoyed seeing me hurt. There were often times I was forced to stand in the corner for what seemed like hours on end. My mom's boyfriend built a small wooden board with a bunch of little pencils on it that I had to stand on while in the corner, and it just hurt my feet so bad. I would be crying, and my mother just turned her head. As long as I was out of their way, it just didn't seem to matter.

One of the worst incidents I recall as a little kid happened while we ate dinner one evening. My mom's boyfriend told me to smell my dinner. It happened to be spaghetti, and when I did, he smashed my face in it and would not let me wipe it off. He thought that was hilarious. I had to sit there and finish eating dinner with all the spaghetti smashed in my face, and he just laughed about it. All the while, my mother allowed this and never spoke up for me. One of his most famous sayings to me was, "You're not even worth the sweat on my balls." As a child, I had no idea what he meant by the comment but knew he was being mean. This is the type of childhood I was living in and dealing with. Years of tears and hurt that would later turn to anger and take root in my heart.

When I was about nine years old, I went to live with my aunt and uncle. I'm not exactly sure why, but I was just sent there to live with them. I thought I had died and gone to heaven. They took care of me. They fed me regularly. They showed me how to be responsible by giving me chores. I absolutely loved living there. They didn't show outward affection, but I just knew they cared about me and loved me.

They called me into the kitchen one day and asked me if I knew what it meant to be adopted. I said no, and they explained it to me. They said that I would stay living with them forever. They would be like my mom and dad, but they would still be my aunt and uncle, and I could see my mother whenever I wanted to. I was very happy about this new arrangement, which lasted only about one year. Then they told me I had to go back and live with my mother and her boyfriend. I'm not exactly sure why, but over the years, my uncle said it all had to do with a $15 a month child-support payment. Today I now understand that the money was the reason and not because they wanted me. My mother's boyfriend would never work a regular job for any length of time. A small job here or there, but it never lasted. They lived off the system, which also explains why we were always moving from place to place.

So here I am, thrown back into this chaotic lifestyle, and now always going to different schools because they were always moving. Of course, the abuse started again. By now, I was about eleven years old. We had moved into a trailer park, and here begins the abuse of sexual molestation by an older kid living nearby. I knew it was wrong and didn't understand it, but he used to give me money and tell me not to tell anybody.

•　　•　　•

The only grandparents I knew were my mother's parents. I never knew my biological father's side of the family. I don't know who my dad is. I have never seen him or known anything about him. No one has ever cared to explain or tell me about these things to this very day. The only way I ever remember my granddad was seeing him paralyzed in bed. When he was a younger man, he got hit in the head in an accident at work, which caused him to have a stroke. So the next twenty years or so of his life he spent in bed or propped in a chair. I loved him a lot and used to go see him all the time to talk and visit or even help him with eating. He was special to me, and I never minded doing for him what I could.

My grandparents lived in a small one-bedroom apartment on the ninth floor in the housing projects. I used to sleep overnight a lot, which would get me away from my mother and her boyfriend. The sad thing about my nanny: She was a kleptomaniac. She provided a lot of things for me and my brothers and sister. Unfortunately, these things were usually stolen. Many times, she got caught and even spent some time in jail.

Another horrible thing she used to do is she would always date Spanish guys while still married to my grandfather. Many times these guys would beat her up. I can recall seeing my nanny covered with black-and-blue marks and with black eyes. She was so beat up and busted up, but she continued to date these men. When I slept over, I used to sleep on the couch, and my nanny had a bed on the other side of the living room. Many nights as I lay on the couch, fifteen to twenty feet away from me my grandma was having sex with these Spanish men, and I hated hearing it. It's very sad and sick, but this is what my childhood memories consist of. This was my childhood "norm" that I grew up in. I didn't understand what all was happening at the time, and I didn't even care too much. All I knew was how glad I was to be away from my mother's house and to not be getting beat by my mom's boyfriend.

•   •   •

As a kid, one of the things I loved to do was play baseball. I was able to sign up on a team in the neighborhood. My Mom never once came to a practice or watched me play. They would never take me; I had to walk, but it was worth it to me because I enjoyed it so much. One day, my mother was taking my brothers and sister to the circus. It happened to be on a baseball practice day, and my mom's boyfriend said I was not allowed to go to the circus with her. She knew how much I wanted to go to the circus and that I had never been before. Mom pulled me aside and told me to go up the street like I was going to baseball practice, and she would meet me at the corner and take me to the circus with the rest of the kids. I was so excited and happy to go, and it was lots of fun. When we got home, her boyfriend found out that I went with her. He made me quit baseball, and I was never allowed to play again because I missed that one practice. I was so hurt, upset, and angry that night. Remembering that incident still bothers me to this day. The one thing I absolutely loved to do was taken away from me. Life never seemed fair to me, and nobody had any regard for me or how I felt about anything. There was no care, no concern, no love, no nothing.

When I was about twelve years old, I was told I could now live with my Uncle Mike, Aunt Carol, and their daughter, my cousin Michelle, for good. It was such a nice life. I had my own bedroom. I was given chores and responsibilities. I was given proper medical attention. I got my teeth fixed. They cared about me like no one ever had before. It was just wonderful to be there with them.

During the year of seventh grade, at school a couple of my buddies and I snuck out to lunch early, and I got caught by the gym teacher. The teacher got very angry and grabbed a hold of me, put my arm behind my back, and slammed me up against the lockers. It really hurt me. I went home and told my aunt and uncle about what had happened. My uncle had an absolute fit about it. He said, "Tomorrow, we're going to school."

We went into the school the next day, and my uncle walked in the office. The office person asked my uncle if he had an appointment. He said, "I don't need an appointment. I want to talk to the gym teacher and the principal right now."

They both came out and went back into the room. I was right outside of the room trying to hear what they were saying.

My uncle told this gym teacher, "I don't manhandle my boy at home. If you ever touch him again, I will come in here and kick your ass. I gave you permission to paddle my boy when he requires discipline, and that's it. You don't ever put your hands on him by manhandling."

I remember thinking, "Wow! He did that for *me*?! What my uncle did that day made me feel like I was really loved. He stuck up for me and defended me, which had never happened in my life before. I felt like I actually mattered! I thought it was so awesome. All the years I lived with my aunt and uncle, I did get disciplined for doing stupid stuff all the time, but they never ever laid a hand on me, not one time. I just love them to death, and I was so very, very thankful that they took me out of the nightmare where I used to live.

•　　•　　•

At sixteen years old, I got caught smoking pot. My aunt and uncle had an absolute fit. They were scared and nervous, and they did not want this to be an influence for their daughter, so I was forced to move back with my mother and her boyfriend. I understand today and don't blame them at all for sending me back. Living back at my mother's, I was very much on guard. Being older and stronger now, I made it clear to my mom's boyfriend that no one was ever, ever going to hit me ever again. I vowed to myself that I would beat him to death if he ever hit me again. My stay there only lasted for maybe nine or ten months when I asked if my aunt and uncle would consider allowing me to come back, and thankfully I was able to move back with them. I was so grateful!

I stayed with them until I was almost twenty years old. I was working a job, partying regularly, enjoying life, and running with my buddies out to all hours of the night drinking. I felt all was going well. I met and was dating a girl steadily for some time, and then came the day she told me she was pregnant. Her parents and my uncle were very angry and upset over the news. My uncle had previously warned me to be smart about girls and dating and all the problems an unwanted pregnancy would cause, and sure enough that is what happened. In my selfishness and ignorance, my first thought and suggestion to my girlfriend was to get an abortion, and I would just pay for it. I told her I never wanted to have children or be a father. She absolutely refused and made it very clear that she wanted to have our baby with or without me. My aunt and uncle were not happy but told me they would be willing to support her but not me and that I must take responsibility and step up. Of course I wanted to do the right thing, so we got married right away. I got some cheap rings and had a quick ceremony with a local minister in the living room and a keg of beer to celebrate—everything was going to be great. I took pride in being a responsible man, always working, and now here I was stepping up and being a husband and father. Drinking was a part of my life and who I was, so I never considered my drinking habits to be any problem because I always did what I was supposed to do. We moved into our own apartment. I worked many hours and made sure the bills got paid, and we began to raise our daughter. I was working a lot to pay for things. We bought a house and life was just moving along. The marriage was good—at least I thought so— but my drinking got worse as time went by. Very often I worked long hours, so I was always taking some kind of drug to stay awake through work. Then I would drink all evening-long with my buddies. *But,* I took care of all my responsibilities—cutting the grass, paying the bills—all the things a responsible person is known for—but only—I did them while drunk.

When I was about twenty-nine years old, I went out to a New Year's Eve party with my wife, and as usual, I got very drunk. When we arrived back home, I got out of the passenger's side door, and because I was so drunk I slammed the door on my hand. In a couple of minutes, my hand swelled up and became gigantic, like Popeye the Sailor. I thought it was funny, and I didn't feel much pain or anything so I just went in to bed. When I woke up the next morning, I was pretty sure there was probably a bunch of broken bones in my hand, so I went to the emergency room.

The doctor took an x-ray and came back and said it was just badly bruised—no broken bones. He also said to me, "I see your left arm was broken, and it was never reset properly."

He showed me the picture on the x-ray, and I could see how the bones grew back together crooked because it had never been properly set. It set off a rage inside me that is hard to explain. I must have been a very small child when my arm was broken, and no one had bothered to take me to a doctor. I was furious and wanted answers. I stole the x-ray when the doctor left the room a short time later and headed out the door.

I confronted my mother about it. She said she knew nothing about it.

I said, "How can a little boy be walking around with a broken arm and nobody knows anything about it?"

I don't remember it, but it was right there in black and white on the x-ray. Somebody broke my arm. My arm got broken somehow! After a lot of yelling and screaming and hollering, my uncle intervened and sternly told me to "Knock it off. That's the end of this."

I ended it, but it only fueled my anger inside, thinking over and over about the many kinds of abuse I suffered as a child, and no one ever cared.

•   •   •

Being a functioning alcoholic, I did a lot of bad things, stupid things, and illegal things the majority of the time. When I was driving, I was under the influence of alcohol, and I messed around with all kinds of illegal drugs. Cocaine was my favorite. I could snort cocaine and continue drinking and drinking.

I was always a good worker; I never missed a day of work. I worked all the overtime they asked me to. I was the employee of the month, employee of the year, and awarded safety award after safety award. Because I looked like the model employee it certainly came as a complete shock to my supervisor at work when I called in and told him that I was quitting and that I had decided I needed to go to rehab.

I was so sick and tired of being drunk, and it just physically and mentally broke me down. I just couldn't take it anymore. As time progressed, my anger also got more and more out of control. I remember driving down the interstate one day, and somebody cut me off. I was so angry I started throwing full cans of beer out of the car window at them. As you can imagine, there are so many stupid things I did. I can't name them all. My rage was so out of control one evening just before I went into rehab; I was out driving around drunk, and somebody pulled out in front of me. It made me so mad, I pulled up and rear-ended the back of his car. The cops came to arrest me, and somehow I managed to talk my way out of it. It was one of four different times I talked my way out of a DUI, which was just terrible because I deserved to be arrested every time. Getting away with breaking the law only made things worse. I felt like a Superman and was untouchable. In truth, my mind was actually out of touch and a complete *mess*!

Reluctantly, my wife got me the appointment to go to rehab. She had heard it all before and had no faith that I had any sincere desire to stop the drinking. I did not realize it, but by this time I had lost all of her respect, and she was sick of it all. Upon going into rehab, I was told by the doctor there that I had no nutrition in my body at all, and this was contributing to my mind not functioning right. I should have been dead. I spent about two weeks in the hospital rehab, and they put me on fluids, nutrition supplements, complete meals, and gave me meds that helped with the alcohol withdrawal. I began to feel much better and stronger. I was really feeling great and knew I was ready to leave and all was good. They told me I was far from being "good" and needed much more rehab, but I did not want to hear of it. I knew what was right for me and signed myself out against their orders. I felt good and was ready to handle life again.

•　　•　　•

My job was there waiting for me, and I thought all was fine and dandy. I found security taking inventory of all I had accomplished, and yet, I was only in my thirties. I had a beautiful wife, a beautiful daughter, a nice home. I had all my toys. I almost had my house paid off, investments in mutual funds; I had nice cars, TVs and VCRs in every room. I had the American dream at a young age, and I was thinking about how great and successful I was. So of course, my drinking was not the problem and it really never was. It was just part of who I was and what I liked to do. That is the mindset that we justify ourselves with. The reality was I had absolutely nothing and was absolutely nothing. My inflated ego refused to acknowledge that I was completely worthless and empty on the inside and was actually a no-good piece of crap... *drunk*! Only my appearance on the outside said that I had it all, and I strutted around as if life just could not be better.

My marriage was falling apart, and I had no clue of the problems that were there because of *me*! I can still remember how it made me sick to my stomach as my wife confronted me with how she felt trying to explain the condition of her life and heart: "I am just dead inside. You never hug me; you never even pay attention to me anymore."

I just laughed it off and felt it was her problem to deal with because she had everything a wife could want, and I had worked myself to death to provide it for her. I never realized that I was the one that caused this emptiness and screwed things up. I had a wife that loved me and put up with my horrible drinking. I had treated her so badly, neglecting her and taking her for granted. It is no wonder why she started to go out to the bars looking for attention and wound up getting a boyfriend that valued her. However, in my drunken stupor, there was no understanding of any truth. Great betrayal and rage is what I felt toward her and her new boyfriend. How could she do this to me after all I had done for her?

The fact of the matter was I had done this to myself. What an incredible hard "pill to swallow," this would be, *but*, by the grace of God, I have been able to get it down today. While still in my drinking mode, I started to do a lot of stupid things in rages of anger, which landed me in jail time after time after time. I knew it was all her fault and that she had done me wrong. It took a while, and God revealed the truth to me that I, myself, had caused all of these problems. If I had not made alcohol my idol and instead been a good husband and a good father, none of this mess would have ever transpired. I can only imagine how my rage and extreme behavior towards her because of what she had done to me had frightened her terribly. My rage and anger landed me in jail four times during the month of April, and I deserved it each time. My whole life was completely flipped upside down. Even so, God knew what he was doing, and His timing is perfect. I landed in jail one last time in May as I was planning to "get even" once and for all. I can still remember the anger, being in that jail cell feeling like a caged animal. It was the worst thing that could ever happen to me in my life. Actually, I was an animal! However, eighteen years later, I can tell you it was the best thing that ever happened to me.

All of this mess that now lives in the past will always be one of the biggest regrets I have in my life. I had a beautiful wife who was a great mother, and I ruined it all because of alcohol. Today, I am glad she knows how sorry I am. I have made amends. I know I'm forgiven, but it still tends to linger in the back of my mind.

•   •   •

The first ten days I spent in the prison, I was in solitary confinement—absolutely horrible. This was the place that my life-altering changes began to take place. I went before the judge and was sentenced to four months in county jail work release with mandatory counseling to include psychological counseling and anger management.

Some folks from a church ministry had been allowed in the jail, and they were offering to take inmates to church if they were interested. I truly didn't want to go and could care less about church, but the other inmates told me I should go because you get a free breakfast. You could eat all you want at breakfast and just lay in a pew during the service and sleep all morning. The thought of a good breakfast and a full belly was enough for me, so I raised my hand and went along. We ate all we wanted, and I was packed up and feeling pretty good, all ready to nap in the pew when the service started. I was just dozing off, and the pastor started to preach the message for that day. I was just half listening as he was talking about relationships and how you treat your family, friends, etc. I felt a bit irritated and just could not take a nap. I started listening and had a desire to hear what that pastor had to say. This was causing a huge stirring in my heart, and I began to think about the kind of person I really was.

I certainly need to mention that somewhere in between jail and being released from counseling in 1997, I am not sure of the exact moment, but Jesus Christ was introduced to me, and I accepted Him as my Lord and Savior. There was a little old man pastor who had come into jail one day and asked if anybody wanted to have church. There is never anything going on in a jail cell, and it certainly seemed like a great way to get some time out, so I raised my hand and went back and talked to the man. He asked me things about me and my goals and plans after I finished my time. I proceeded to tell him all the plans I had to get my revenge on those that did me wrong. I didn't hold back a thing and told him some pretty scary stuff, but that man never blinked an eye. His only response to me as he opened his Bible was, "Well now, let's see what God has to say about that." He read out loud a verse that has forever stayed with me:

Romans 12:19: "Do not take revenge, my dear friends, but leave room for God's wrath, for it is written: 'it is mine to avenge; I will repay,' says the Lord."

This was definitely a changing point in my life. I didn't know it then, but I sure do know it now.

My initial counseling session did not go well at all. There was a big disagreement and argument with the counselors. It was evident to me that they were more concerned with getting their payments than helping me. I hated the people there and refused to go back. I didn't think I needed to go in the first place. When it was time for my second counseling session, my parole officer met with me to remind me that I was court ordered to go and that I would be put back in jail if I refused. I told him, "If I have to go back there, I will show you how to kill a person with my bare hands," and at the time I meant every word. This was the point I had gotten to in my life: I had a destructive rage, anger, and hatred for everything, everyone, and for the entire world. Everyone had done me wrong!

My parole officer called me back to tell me he had another place he wanted me to go to for counseling, and he boldly told me, "You *must* go."

So off I went to the new counseling place with a huge chip on my shoulder. I just knew this was all about the money and that they could care less about me. It was one man and one woman counselors, and they told me that they were there to help me. I told her right to her face, "You are full of crap. All you want is the money."

That counselor said something to me that stuck with me to this day. He said to me, "A lot of your problems and your actions are because you were raised in a dysfunctional home environment and were never taught properly, and that is not your fault." He continued, "Our job is to teach you the right way to live and experience life." I never really thought about how I was taught anything in my life; I always managed to survive doing things my own way. Anyone could see that didn't work out very well.

After about three months of sitting there at my sessions just putting my time in, doing nothing with what they were trying to teach me because I was convinced it was all a big waste of time and money, the counselor pulled me aside and told me that there was a small but very important attachment to my court order that said that if I did not make progress, I was not allowed to leave counseling. The only way I was allowed to be released from their program was by a letter from them to the judge declaring I had made improvements in my life. I didn't want to stay in this program forever and go broke paying the fees, so I began to take things a bit more seriously. I started to participate in class, doing some of the things they had explained to me about turning my life around. These were huge, huge changes; from getting new clothes, to associating with different friends, to the way I spoke, the way I looked, the way I talked to people, and changing my thinking, behavior, and actions towards others.

Within two months, I found myself raising my hand in this class wanting to participate in the little activities. They did the little skits that help you practice proper reactions to real-life situations, and I learned a lot. I mean, *a lot*! After about three months, I was informed that they saw definite progress in me and that they had written a letter to the judge. I was thrilled to finally be released from counseling as well as that weekly payment! It was then that my counselor emphasized to me that, "You will only be completing half the course. We think this would be good for you and a great benefit to your life if you continue on your own for the next six months to completion."

My response was, "Screw you. I'm gone and not doing any more of this!" So I walked out feeling pretty good that all this counseling stuff was finally over. When the next Tuesday evening session time came around, I was at my apartment with my buddy relaxing. I had the strangest feeling come over me, like somebody was pushing me, telling me I needed to go back to counseling. It was such a strong feeling that I could not make sense of it, but that "push" was so big I decided to go back, and I continued for the next six months. Today, I know that that "push" was the Holy Spirit working in me, and I am so thankful I listened to that "push"! I paid for each session as before, and I finished the course, which was a whole year program, and to this day, it has benefited me greatly.

After I was released from jail and my counseling, God started to put my life back in order. I did not know it at the time, but as I look back and reflect on it, I can see how God was working everything out for good, even when I was in jail.

Thankfully, I had retained my job throughout the jail work-release program and was able to get myself a small apartment. I was still in the process of going through a horrible divorce, losing all my "stuff," and an awful lot of money. Anger continued to be a problem for me, but God kept me focused, and I began to accept the reality that my drinking and behavior was the cause. I started going to AA meetings while in work release and continued going on a very regular basis. Sometimes I would go to two meetings a day. This sober living was my priority and focus, and I was willing to do whatever it took to stay sober. AA holds a special place in my heart to this very day. The program works 100 percent of the time if you truly want sobriety and *do the program.*

When I first got out of jail, one of the things I was told to do was to find a church to join and become a member. So I attended what looked like a nice church that was close by my apartment. Walking into the church that first day, I was really shocked at how people treated me. Only a few people would say "Hello," and many just stared at me. It was easy to see and feel their eyes of judgment upon me by their cold glances and lack of friendliness toward me. Overall, it made me feel like I didn't belong there, but I didn't give up. I continued to go but never felt right there, so I was still searching for the right place.

A friend of a friend invited me to go to their small church and said how "different" they were and that I would feel comfortable there, so I gave it a try. Sunday morning I met my friend there, and as soon as I walked in the front door, I felt something in that place. I didn't know what it was, but it felt right. People were friendly, they came up and talked to me and introduced themselves. At that moment, I felt it was the place I was supposed to be.

I continued attending that small church, and I started to develop a relationship with two people. One being Pastor Mitch and the other a man I call "Moe," who had a past life of addiction and pain, much like my own. I didn't know at the time how important these men would become in my life, but God sure did! They took me under their wing. They mentored me and taught me so much. I see today how God placed these men in my life and worked through them to get me "rooted" in God's Holy Word. A men's small group Bible study began at Moe's house every week that lasted over five years. The value and impact that this small group Bible study had on me has been incredible. Unfortunately, like many small churches, there were growing disagreements among certain groups of people in the congregation that led to a falling away, and the doors were shut. Pastor Mitch moved on to another ministry in another state. Before leaving, he stressed to me that I needed to continue in church and to not stop going. I had no idea where to begin to search for another church that would help me grow in my walk. He told me to search for a Bible-based church. "To find a church that has the word Bible in it or Baptist and start going there." But the important thing that he made clear to me was to continue going to church and continue walking with God because without God I could easily fall back into my old destructive habits. Mitch moved away, but I still keep in contact with him to this day. I still live close to Moe, and he continues mentoring me to this day.

I started going to a Baptist church, and it was good. I learned a lot, made some good friends, and continued to grow and learn about Jesus and how to apply it to my life.

Probably about two or three years after being sober, this is about 2000 or 2001, I got married again. I was told by many, many people not to do it, to continue to work on myself, but I didn't listen to them. Unfortunately, the marriage only lasted a couple of years, and we both went our separate ways, and that was the end of that.

Even so, I kept after my relationship with God. Reading my Bible, growing to learn, and understanding and going to church. Not understanding everything, only understanding a little, I know that this clean and sober living by walking with God was the way, and I wanted to live it.

Some seventeen or eighteen years later, life still came with all its problems and hassles, but I continued to walk with God. He helped me each day working through my resentment problems, forgiveness problems, and anger problems, and things started to get better a little at a time.

Something I do want to make very clear: After I got out of jail and was clean and sober, you will notice that I refer back to God. I want to make this very, very clear that the God I am talking about is the God of the Bible, the creator of Heaven and Earth; the God in the Bible who sent His son, who was conceived by the Holy Spirit and born of a virgin, who lived a perfect life with no sin and was crucified on the cross, was dead, was buried, and after three days arose alive and was seen by many, many people to prove He was the Son of God, the Savior of the world, and that be believing in Him, you may have eternal life. So when you see me mention the word God, you can refer back to this statement.

For about two years, I stayed single and focused on God, work, and living a sober life. I began to give some thought to maybe meeting someone nice. I had been pushing myself with a schedule of just working, working, and working, and whatever free time I had was spending time with my niece, nephew, and granddaughter. I thought it would probably be best if I just stayed single for the rest of my life, but I did start to get a little lonely. It would be nice to have a companion friend to go out and have dinner with; not a man but a female. So anyway, I said I'd give the online dating a try.

I worked third shift and slept half the day, so it was going to have to be somebody who was willing to work with me around my schedule if I was ever going to get involved with them. I was very skeptical about this online dating thing, anyway. I thought I would try it. I talked to some of my buddies at work, and they said, "You just have to be aware and careful who you talk to because there can be some strange people out there."

I signed up on one of the popular paying sites and set up my profile. It was very interesting seeing so many people out there looking for that special someone. You just have no idea what they are really about, so reading about them and chatting can become rather exhausting. I clicked on this profile of a Christian woman who today is my beautiful, awesome wife and best friend in the world. We met for the first time for lunch at a restaurant and chatted for a few hours. I felt things went very well. When we ordered lunch, I asked her if it was okay to pray. I had made it very clear in the profile I set up I was not interested in a one-night stand. I was interested in a long-term relationship, and first and foremost, you need to know who Jesus Christ is. I did find out later that she really thought I was trying to put on a "show" of how I was such a good Christian and that she had huge doubts about my character. For probably the first six months of dating, she was very unsure about me. She had been through a difficult and abusive past and it was difficult for her to trust men. As time went on, she came to realize that I was a sincere man and that she could let her guard down. We really "clicked" in so many ways. A dear friend told me that you know when you have found your true "soul mate" when you both just "Click". We probably dated for about two years before we got married. Even today, six years later, it is still the same. She is just an awesome woman and my true soulmate.

●　　　●　　　●

It was May 2012. Memorial Day weekend was approaching, and the weather was really getting nice. I put my motorcycle in the shop, got a complete tune up and brand new tires; everything was ship-shape. I was ready for the three-day weekend. What a story from that day forward!

That Memorial Day weekend, I remember the excitement of spring and motorcycle riding weather in the air. I worked the night shift through the week, and when I got in Saturday morning, I didn't go to sleep as I usually did because the day was just awesome. I cut the grass, did some weed-whacking, and went out on my Harley, riding all day long. I came home that evening and went to bed. Sunday morning we went to church, went out to eat, took a little bit of a nap, and worked around the house. I knew I hadn't really "caught up" on my sleep, but I was energized knowing I had the long weekend to play. Monday was beautiful, and I was determined to ride my motorcycle all day again and break in my new tires while having some fun. I drove everywhere, stopping and visiting some friends and never taking a break, only grabbing a coffee here and there.

I had been pushing myself to the limit and recall being pretty tired when my wife called at around seven o'clock to see when I was heading home.

I was at my brother's apartment about an hour away and told her I would be heading out shortly. I started down the interstate, and that is the last thing I remember. I am pretty sure I fell asleep while riding my motorcycle.

From the police statements and eyewitnesses that reported my accident, I was traveling at a high rate of speed and for no apparent reason I just veered off the side of the road into the median strip. They reported that alcohol was a factor in this crash, insisting they smelled it at the scene where I had vomited on impact. This was a complete lie that was set straight six to seven months after my accident. I personally submitted my blood-test results from the medical center that I was flown into that night after the accident, and they indicated there were no drugs or alcohol in my system. The Police Department refused to change the report and only attached my records to it. I am happy to set this record straight today.

When I hit the median strip, which thankfully was all grass, there was a slight embankment that I hit, and I was thrown off my motorcycle, airborne across a bridge, and I landed approximately forty-five feet away in a grassy area on the other side. The motorcycle hit the bridge and fell, landing on the street below the interstate. I was not wearing my helmet that day.

The Life Lion Helicopter flew me to the medical center, where I was found to have horrendous injuries and brain trauma and was not expected to live. The news report that evening stated that I was, "not yet deemed a fatality."

The list of injuries was extreme. I was in a coma and put on life support upon arrival. I had a brain injury called a diffuse axonal, which is when your brain is literally bounced around so much there are internal tears from inside your head. I had brain bleeding and was told that my head had swelled so severely my eyes had disappeared, looking like lines on my face. I had a broken neck, nose, and shoulder-blade, and several ribs on the left side of my rib cage were broken, and my right foot was shattered. My pelvis was broken in the front and the back, requiring immediate surgery. That's why today I still have a big bolt the whole way through my pelvis holding me together.

I was in a coma for six days, on life support and not expected to survive due to the nature and damage of the injuries. Because my brain injury was the most traumatic and damaging, a censor was placed in my skull to monitor any swelling. If it swelled, they would have to do emergency surgery to relieve the pressure. The doctors explained to my wife and sister that due to the brain bleeds and tissue tearing in multiple areas, it would never heal to reconnect correctly within the brain and would leave me severely impaired. If I were to survive, I would be in a vegetative state, completely dependent for care. I would not even know my name or recognize people.

As I am told, my immediate family, pastor, and church family began a prayer chain and came many times to my bedside and gathered at the shock-trauma center in constant prayer over the situation. I was placed completely in Almighty God's hands. My pastor, Howard Edmondson, and his wife Wanda, came in to pray over me. Pastor knew I loved the Lord and prayed that God would not let me suffer and to take me home. As they were praying, they noticed a tear had rolled out of my eye and down my cheek. He said to his wife, "He can hear me!" God spoke to him in that moment and told him, "Pray for this man to be healed. He is going to get up and walk again," and that's what he prayed over me. I feel strongly that this pertains to Scripture that says, "My sheep hear my voice and know me." My pastor and dear friend is my earthly shepherd.

The whole time in shock trauma, the nurses would come in several times a day to do pain checks to see if I would respond to pain and show brain activity. They would grab, twist, and pinch my skin very hard on my chest to try to get some kind of physical movement that would show my brain was acknowledging the pain. If I moved, it would indicate that my brain was functioning by sending signals causing my arms to react from the pain. The nurse explained to my wife that it is like when you get stung by a bee; your brain tells your arm to swat it off. There was never any response, but my wife tells me my chest had black and blue marks all over it. They sure tried many, many times over.

After the sixth day in the trauma center, I still showed no signs of brain activity or improvement. It was a Sunday morning when the doctors told my wife and sister that due to complications and infection from being on life support, a decision had to be made by Monday. Do they want them to proceed and continue my care with life support or remove it? In order for me to continue on life support, they would need to perform the surgery for a permanent tracheotomy as well as insert a feeding tube. The alternative was to remove me from life support altogether. My wife and sister knew I would never have wanted to live in such a state. Both, with broken hearts, agreed to take me off of life support. I cannot even imagine how difficult this must have been. They asked the doctor if removal could be delayed until Tuesday. This would give my coworkers, close family, and friends the chance to come and say their goodbyes. The following is an account of what happened in those few days, as was told to me by my wife, sister, pastor, and church family who witnessed God's hand of divine intervention.

Some of my co-workers came in that Sunday afternoon and many people had been in and out all day. My wife stayed by my side almost 24/7 since the day of the accident, praying and constantly looking for signs of brain activity. The nurses would get annoyed with her because she would ask them to keep doing the "pain checks" on me. She was told gently to not "get any hopes up; a brain injury like this never has a good ending."

It was now Sunday evening, and my wife was in the waiting room with her parents who had come to see me, when the evening nurse came out and asked her to come with her to my room. Walking back to my room, the nurse said she wanted to show her something she may want to see. At my bedside, the nurse firmly grabbed my broken shoulder, squeezing it, and grabbed a chunk of skin on my chest and twisted really hard. At that moment, my left hand lifted up about two inches toward hers. The nurse said "There! Now I can rate him for response on a scale that indicates brain activity." My wife burst out in tears and ran out to get her parents to witness it. They praised God and called everyone to tell them the news. Even more prayers for my healing were now being lifted up to the Lord. I was so black and blue after that night!

There was quite a stirring in the shock trauma unit over the next few days as my movements and responding began to increase. I was getting the attention of many of the staff and doctors in the unit, who became very interested in the changes going on with my condition. By Monday morning, there were signs on the respiratory monitor that I was trying to breathe on my own. It was then decided by the doctors to leave me on the ventilator to see if I would continue to progress and start to wake up.

The nurses would then periodically come in my room and call my name loudly while shaking my shoulder and saying "Wake up." By Monday evening, my family was going wild, clapping and praising God in the shock trauma unit as my eyes started to respond and open ever so slightly, and I was squeezing hands when asked. God Almighty had been performing miracles right before everyone's eyes. My wife and family all knew it was God moving, yet the hospital staff and doctors would hear nothing of it. My wife told me how the nurses insisted she should not get any hope up. They sternly stressed to her that I may regain consciousness but would likely have no ability to understand, read, or write, and may not even know her name. I continued to become more alert each day while still on the life support ventilator. I could follow people with my eyes and move my fingers and toes when asked. My wife came in the next Thursday afternoon determined to prove to the nurses and staff wrong. She quietly, without a word, held up a large sign in front of me that read:

IF YOU CAN READ THIS, NOD YOUR HEAD YES

I nodded my head "yes," and she started crying and ran out to the nurses' station to tell them that I had just read and understood the sign. God was healing me, yet their reaction was clear that they were not buying it! Even so, the events sure made me a popular patient that week. There were groups of doctors that would come to my room just to see me. One of the trauma center staff nurses told my wife that the man they were seeing clinically with these injuries is not the same man they were seeing in that hospital bed. I continued to progress. God is so awesome!

After coming out of the coma, I was taken off the ventilator and was now breathing on my own. I actually don't recall many of these details because my brain was actually in a "fog" and I was a bit confused, but each day more clarity would come. Next was surgery to repair my shattered foot, and then I was transferred over to the brain/spine injury rehabilitation hospital where I would live for another month or so. I was unable to move around in the bed and could not use my arms or hands. My bed was equipped with a blow-tube device that was attached to the bed rail. Whenever I needed help I had to blow in the tube that would turn on the nurse call-light in the hallway. I was so frustrated, being in this helpless and hopeless state and in constant pain. I started wondering how awful life was going to be for me. I was completely paralyzed lying in a bed. I started praying to God, but I became very angry at the same time. One evening after my wife left, I got to thinking of how close to dying I had been after the accident and that I could have been in heaven with my Lord and Savior instead of being in this hospital bed all mangled up. I became so mad and angry I started yelling and screaming out loud at God, demanding Him to tell me "Why would you let me live? Why would you let me live? Why?!" The nurse in the hallway overheard my outburst and assumed I was on the phone yelling at my wife. The nurse approached my wife the next day when she came in to visit and asked if I was yelling at her last evening on the phone. The nurse told my wife that regardless of my injuries, she should never take such abuse from me. My wife had no idea what that nurse was referring to, as we have never argued. She even checked the front desk roster to see if someone had been in to visit with me that that evening, but there were no visitors that whole day.

The next morning when I woke up, God spoke to me, but not in a verbal way; it was like a very strong impression in my mind coming from within. God said, "I have work for you to do."

I said out loud, "Father, what kind of work do you have for me to do? I'm paralyzed in this bed. I can't feed myself, drink from a cup, or even go to the bathroom by myself. I have to blow in a hose and call a nurse just to get help." I was so frustrated and stressed that I could do nothing to change my circumstance.

During this entire ordeal, God was making sure I was being humbled down to nothing. I was totally dependent on everyone to do everything for me. I needed assistance for every little thing: bathing, toileting, brushing my teeth, scratching an itch, feeding, getting dressed, blowing my nose, or just turning on the TV or changing the channel. I could not even hold a pen to write, so I had to just mark an "X" instead of signing paperwork while there. God began a work in my life in a way I could never have imagined. I was learning to be totally dependent on *Him*. With therapy, I eventually was able to sit up and was in a wheelchair, although I still was dependent on the nurses to pick me up and set me in the wheelchair. Slowly, with therapy, things started to progress. I gained the ability to move my arms better. I had a thick plastic neck brace for my broken neck for nine weeks. It was horrible. I still have the scars today from the device cutting and slicing into my neck. On the actual night of my accident, the doctors had surgically placed metal bars into my pelvic bones that came out through my skin and connected to a large bar that ran across the front of me called a fixator. It is a kind of metal cage designed to help hold the pelvis in place so that it doesn't move throughout the healing process. It did not allow me to move much, and of course I was bedridden until they would surgically remove it.

After a few days in the rehab, I had become more alert and able to move and was able to shift myself around better in bed to get comfortable, but I still was not able to get up. One morning, instead of calling for help to grab something from the floor, I made the mistake of leaning out over the side of the bed a bit too far and snapped one of the internal bolts that went down into my pelvis. It sounded like a gunshot when it broke, but I did not feel any pain. That situation resulted in a lengthy, difficult operation to get that threaded bolt out, since they had to literally "dig" into my pelvic bone to remove it. What an ordeal!

While in the rehab hospital, I was ordered to receive cognitive rehabilitation. Apparently brain injuries as severe as mine required this to determine my level of need and care. But in my particular case, God had miraculously intervened in the healing of my brain, which made this therapy pretty frustrating for me. Every time I met with the therapist, she would ask me my name, where I lived, and the name of the hospital. She would ask me when I was born, what my wife's name was, and where I was employed. Did I have a daughter? What was her name? What was my granddaughter's name? I was so sick and tired of repeating myself over and over each time. I became so irritated and yelled at the woman saying, "*Oh* my *gosh*, are you people crazy?! Why on earth do you keep asking me the same questions day after day?"

The therapist then explained to me how my injuries were so severe and extreme that I was not supposed to be alive. I was not supposed to be able to talk or communicate. Based on all my scans and charts, my brain should not be able to function or process information as a normal person. I should not be able to remember things, have insight, understand, or even be aware of what is going on. At the time, I didn't realize these things from a medical perspective, but I do today. I can only look up and smile and embrace the *miracle* God has done in my life. My injuries were so severe, the doctors are still amazed that I am able to speak, think, and remember and that I and am completely functional. Since day one of my accident, people from all over town had been praying for my healing and lifting me up to the Lord. Prayers from friends, family, and other churches—from people I have never known. Even a church in Africa had me on their prayer chain. I am a walking testimony of God's miracle of healing, which He chose to do within me, as well as a testimony of the power of prayer in these circumstances.

Remembering this still leaves me speechless and in *awe*!

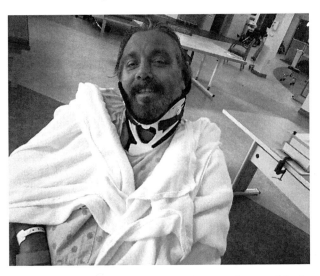

Rehab begins after 1 ½ months in a hospital bed

•   •   •

Physical therapy was a long, grueling process. My assigned therapist was a young lady who had just finished up her studies. She was doing an internship for her final grade, and I was her newest patient. My body was a mess from being bed-ridden for so long. I had to start learning how to use my muscles all over again, from walking to moving my arms and buttoning my shirt. It was just a grueling thing. This young lady was just awesome. She was patient, kind, and caring, but she also didn't let me get away with anything. God put her in place to work with me, and I will never forget the impact she had in my healing process. I have stopped back and visited many times and thanked her so much.

Being unable to get out of bed to use the bathroom, I had a catheter in place for just over a month. I can laugh now thinking of this, but it wasn't funny at the time. When on a catheter for so long, it makes your muscle reflexes soft, and they don't want to work. So after they took the catheter out, my bladder wouldn't work. Every day, for five times a day, the nurses would come in and do an ultrasound on my stomach to see how full my bladder was, and they would have to use a catheter to empty my bladder. Oh what fun this was. It went on for about six days straight. Finally, when my bladder started to work on its own, I had no control to stop it. I rang for the nurse and told her about the mess that I had just made.

She kindly told me, "Don't worry about it."

After about four or five days, I was able to go to the bathroom on my own. You have no idea how happy I was to be able to go to the bathroom; we actually celebrated the event. God certainly stripped me of any pride through this ordeal!

Well, God had another miracle to show the doctors. An MRI of my head and neck was done, and I was scheduled to have two bones fused to repair my broken neck. My surgeon went to perform the surgery and discovered that the bones had already fused themselves in the exact same place he was going to fuse them. The two-hour surgery lasted just forty minutes, and he closed me up and called my wife to tell her how remarkable my healing was. All kinds of praises and shouts of glory went up to Almighty God that day.

It was about three weeks before I was getting ready to get out of the rehab facility and go home. Words could never express the excitement and emotion that stirred in me anticipating the day I would be going home. Rehab therapists told me I had to be able to stand on my own and transfer to a wheelchair before they would release me. I felt I was ready and that it would be a piece of cake. This would be the first time I was going to stand up and try to walk since my accident three months before. When they helped me stand, holding onto the parallel bars, it was very weird and strange. I was extremely dizzy and felt very weak. A couple times, I had to sit back down in the wheelchair. With the help of the aides, I was held up in a standing position for a minute that felt like an hour. I was using all the strength within me to stand, and I began to shake uncontrollably. It was scary and very emotional for me that day, and it completely exhausted me. How was I going to walk on my own again? Would I ever be able to work again? I was filled with anxiety and uncertainty. I just refused to live being dependent on others. More than ever, I was determined to get out of that wheelchair and walk again. I prayed and stayed focused on my therapy day after day to get strong enough to go home.

My doctor came in one morning making his rounds, and he knew I would be heading home in the next few days. We had a one-on-one discussion about my future and about everything that had happened to that point. He knew my anxiety and that the long road I had ahead was not going to be easy. He left me with this very encouraging story:

> *There's an old farmhouse in the middle of the field. It's been there for at least two-hundred years. One day, a huge tornado and hurricane came through the land and ripped the farm to pieces. Tore the roof off, tore the front door off, ripped the windows out, and knocked the chimney over. This farmhouse was in terrible shape. When the construction company came to look over the damage on the farmhouse, they said, "We're*

going to rebuild. We're going to put a new room on, new windows, and new chimney, fix the front sidewalk, and fix all the damage done. The farmhouse will never ever be the same, but it will be able to function and operate as a nice little cozy farmhouse. But it will never be the original farmhouse that was built two-hundred years ago. Your body is this farmhouse. Remember this: it's never going to be the way it was before this, but we're about rebuilding your body and making changes and working with it. You will be okay. It's never going to be like the old body, but it will be okay. You will be able to function and live.

A very cool doctor he is. I still stop back to see him once or twice a year.

I finally got to go home, I was absolutely overwhelmed. Alone, sitting in my own living room after my visitors and family that helped me settle in had gone home, I pondered what had happened over the last three to four months of my life. The help and encouragement that I received from family and friends and my dear church family was incredible. My little buddies from Sunday school, the boys and girls, were always mailing me cards and telling me to get well. It just overwhelmed me. When I came home, everybody was still so supportive of me. My buddies I used to ride motorcycles with got together and all went on a ride to raise money to help out with the enormous medical bills. About thirty or more motorcycles pulled up in front of my house late one Sunday afternoon. I was overwhelmed; it just made me cry. My wife set up a charity benefit to raise money for further help with the doctor bills and medical bills. My family, friends, and church family helped so much to care for me. They took me to doctor appointments and picked me up, dragging my wheelchair all around. People brought meals to the house. A dear neighbor was always taking the time to check in on me throughout the day while my wife worked. It is just amazing how God provided for me through these people.

•　　•　　•

Here's a copy of an essay that my nephew wrote telling the story of my accident as a part of a school assignment. I think it is very cool because this is from an eleven-year-old boy who I have been very close to since the day he was born. It breaks my heart that this young man had come to say goodbye to his uncle because he was going to die. I love him very much, and I know how much he loves me. It's so very special, and I just want to share.

Garret Bretz
Narrative Essay
10-22-14

The Crash That Could Have Ended It All

"Hello ma'am, im sorry to tell you that Calvin Shatto has been in a really bad motorcycle accident. He was going about 100 mph. and hit a barrier, flew over a highway and landed on the road." The next thing, I was over in her room crying. "What happened?" I said as she was getting ready to go. "Just get your clothes on and go down stairs.

When we all got down there she was talking to my dad. "'Calm down and tell me what is happening."

"Mikie is in the hospital because of a motorcycle accident and he isn't looking like he is going to make it."

"He's what?" I yell at the top of my lungs.

"Its going to be okay Garret, just keep praying, and that I did. When everyone got down there my mom told us that my Uncle Mikie has been in a really bad motorcycle accident and that we were going to see him. As expected everybody started to cry.

It took about an hour to get there and when we did it took another half hour to get to his room. Before we went in we stopped at the desk to make sure he was in that room.

"Excuse me, is this the room that Calvin Shatto is in? My mom asked as the lady looked up.

"Yea but you he isn't looking so good."

"We'll still go in."

We went in to see him in a coma. He looked terrible and i couldn't bare to look at him. I started crying (and so did everyone else that was in the room) and I ran out of the room.

The next day we went back and they told us that he was not going to make it. They told us that we could decide if we want to keep him breathing or take the machine out. We told them to take it put, but they said they are not aloud to until night.

We went home and hours later they called and said that he started breathing on his own and he might live. Hearing that I made my mom drive us to the hospital right away and she was happy to do that. When we got there the doctors would not let us in there no matter what. They were trying to take the breathing tube out.

"When can we go in out." I asked my mom.

"Whenever they tell us we can."

"Hey mom, do you think he is going to be okay?"

"As I keep saying I hope so and just keep on praying and he might." That ended our conversation because I was falling asleep, It was 3:00 in the morning.

When I woke up It was 1:00 in the afternoon and still nothing about my uncle. I went up to the lady sitting at the desk and asked her if I could go in and see him but instead of her saying no she let me in. As soon as I walked in it felt different in the room then it did the day before, it felt like hope.

This same routine went on for days and days and days. Finally about two weeks after he started breathing on his own almost all of his bones healed. This was an answer of prayer. Almost all of his were broken and they healed this fast, it was a MIRACLE.

About one more week later he started to wake up, again it was MIRACLE. He would sometimes move his fingers or toes or even blink to let you know he understood. Soon after that he could almost talk. I went in one day and talked to him.

"Uncle Mikie, are you awake?"

"Yeah hey buddy what's going on?"

"Nothing I just came to check on you and maybe talk if you're feeling up to it."

"Yeah I am."

"Do you remember why you went that fast, especially without a helmet?"

"I really dont know im sorry." And of course the nurse told me to leave and that he had to go to sleep. I told him bye and that I love him and left.

It went on like this for a few weeks going back and forth. Finally they told him he had to go to a rehab (rehabilitation center) and he couldn't go home until he could walk fully again. He went there and he did not start working out yet because one of the only broken bones left in his body was his neck.

His neck did not heal for about 2 months. But when it did he was ready to get started working out to get out of that place. He had to start lifting 5 pound weights and walking with a walker. It was not fun to watch because he Was in pain for most of it. It took very many long, long months untill he finally got done with it.

To this day he is alive and moving. The doctors said that he was going to die but he fought through and made it out alive. He is still getting surgerys and going to the hospital to get shots and will have to for a while.

He does not remember why he did it and he probably never will. He should not have been going 100 mph. in the first place let alone without wearing a helmet. Remember to wear a helmet every time you ride your bicycle, motorcycle, or even when you're riding a scooter. It could affect your life and others.

•   •   •

I was really making progress with physical therapy and trying to move from needing a wheelchair to using a walker to get around. I went to physical therapy twice a week, every single week, and suddenly got a letter in the mail that the insurance was not going to pay for my physical therapy any more. The letter said that based on their information, I no longer require therapy. I cannot tell you how upset and furious I became. It was like being punched in the stomach.

Fortunately, the staff at my physical therapy center helped to calm my nerves and explained how this is a very common occurrence that insurance companies do all the time. Sure, I could find a lawyer and try to go that route, but there are no guarantees, and in the time it would take I would certainly wind up back in the wheelchair.

The owner of the physical therapy business, Sarah, said, "You need to come for another two months. You just pay what you can because I don't want to see you go back in a wheelchair. With continued therapy and another two months, you will be walking with a cane. Another six months from now you won't even use a cane."

I've got to give a holler out to Sarah, who God also set before me. She is awesome, awesome, awesome! She cares about her patients and wants to see them succeed. She was not in business just for the money; it is about people. As time progressed, I learned a lot about these insurance companies, and I don't have anything good to say about them. They treat people wrongly, and that is the truth. When you have serious problems, and you have very expensive medical bills or property damage, they manipulate the system and will not pay. I bought and paid for long-term insurance, and they just decided to stop coverage and refuse to pay. I say this to alert everybody about it. The system is beyond broken. However, God is in control!

I continued in therapy for a few months, and by the grace of God, I was able to walk out that door using just my cane. This was an incredible accomplishment from where I had been. The road was still long and difficult because of all the injuries, but my focus was on just getting through one day at a time. During a service in church one Sunday morning, a very dear friend and sister-in-Christ, Miss Anna Blake, leaned up behind me and whispered, "I know you're in a lot of pain." I am sure it was quite noticeable as I hobbled in each week.

I said, "Yes, I sure am."

She said, "I'm also in a lot of pain."

I said, "What is your pain from?"

She said, "I've had five hip replacements."

I said, "Oh my goodness gracious are the doctors doing something wrong? What's the problem?"

She said, "The parts that they are putting in keep going bad. Mike, I know about all of your pain from all the surgeries and all the nerves being cut. Let me tell you this. You keep a good attitude, you keep smiling, and you keep chugging along, because that's just the way it is."

Those were just a few words of encouragement that I have told many, many times to other people, and those are the words of encouragement that I will take to my grave.

Unfortunately, just a few months later, Miss Anna had to have an emergency operation on her stomach. I went to the hospital to see her and was amazed. Just about ten hours after surgery, and she was sitting up in the chair talking to me. She was somewhere around seventy-five to eighty years old, in excellent shape, and in pretty good condition. I always thought it was very, very cool when her husband Larry came in to see her. Every time those two would come together, they would always greet each other with a kiss, even after about forty years of marriage—that is so cool!

Maybe a week later during a test, they found out that Miss Anna had a type of ovarian cancer that could not be cured because the previous operation had not healed yet. Her husband called me and told me she may only have about two weeks to live. I went to see Mrs. Anna; I was very distraught, just realizing that her time on earth may not be long. I asked her about the cancer.

She said, "Here's the way it is, Mike. I will deal with this operation to get it healed up first. Then we'll deal with the cancer." She had a great attitude. She had a smile on her face. She said, I'll just keep chugging along because that's just the way it is."

This woman had just been handed her death sentence in about two weeks, and she had the same attitude that she lived with, even in the face of death. She knew she was going to go be with her Lord and Savior.

Approximately two weeks later, she did go home to be with the Lord. I had the honor and privilege to spend about two hours with her while she was in hospice. This dear lady is and always will remain an inspiration to me, and I will carry her story on to help and inspire other people as long as I live.

•   •   •

As I come to the end of the adventure of writing a book about my life, this is where I am today in 2019. My circumstances did not limit what God still had in store for me.

I live each day with all kinds of aches and pains. I move slowly some days. I get very fatigued, and some days I nap quite a bit, which is part of the brain injury. I have days when I am full of anxiety and feel like I'm crawling out of my skin. I'm getting ready to go to the doctors in order to get some medication for that. I also want to see if they have some type of medication for all the aches and pains, arthritis, and joint pain that I have. I can still hear Miss Anna telling me, "It's just the way it is, Mike." Regardless of my physical pain, it cannot take away from the peace in my heart that God has given me. The kind of work God has me doing for Him today is just so awesome. I'm dumbfounded and humbled at how he uses me. When there are new Christians coming in to church, I get together with them and mentor them, whether by words of encouragement, getting them a new Bible, explaining things to them, or just talking to them on the phone, saying "Hello, how are you doing?" I have been involved with recovery houses where people with addictions go to try to get clean and sober and get their lives on track because I have lived that lifestyle.

God is using me to help people, teach them, encourage them, and take them by the hand and show them what they need to do to live a clean and sober life. Unfortunately, most don't want to do what is necessary in order to stay clean and sober. My main concern is to point them to Jesus, who can guide and direct them to what they need to do to stay clean and sober; God will do the rest if they let Him. At my church I feel very blessed to serve however I can: help out here and there, be a greeter or an usher once a month. I help count the offering. I teach an adult Bible study every other Friday night, which is just absolutely awesome. Everybody in the group is learning. I am learning, and we are growing in the knowledge of God. He has made it an awesome little group. I still teach Sunday school about every third Sunday. I get great joy out of interacting with the children, teaching them, explaining Scripture, being their friends and developing relationships with them, and sometimes discussing life issues with them—it's very fulfilling for me.

About two years ago, I was asked if I would be a deacon at church. I said, "No, all that may do is make me have a big, fat head, thinking that I'm somebody when I'm nobody."

I didn't think it would be a good fit for me because pride can be an ugly, ugly thing. I spoke to a friend of mine about my concern, and he explained to me: "Throw out the word deacon. What you are is a servant of God. Nothing more than a servant." That really put it into perspective for me, and I said, "Okay, I'll do it."

What a joy it is to serve a living God! Some of the things that deacons do are visit people in hospitals, encourage people, call people, and check up on people. I have visited a few people in the hospital who have been in horrible accidents. I can easily connect with those I visit in the hospital. The average person doesn't understand what it's like unless you've been in a horrible accident or had to spend a lot of time in a hospital bed. It's just so cool and amazing how God uses people and how God is using me.

I want to make something very, very clear. It is only by God's grace and mercy that He has shined upon me that I am where I am in life today, and I assure you, I do not deserve it. All the hurt, pain, and feelings of complete hopelessness that I experienced throughout my life were worth it all to bring me to knowing Jesus Christ as my Lord and Savior.

When you come before God with a sincere heart and you say, "Jesus, I accept you as my Lord and Savior. I want you to change my life. I don't know what I should do. I don't know what I'm doing, but I know I want to follow you. I believe what you did on the cross for me. I believe in the virgin birth, that you died, and I believe in your resurrection."

The important thing is that when believe and say these things to God, you mean it from the bottom of your heart, with sincerity. I assure you, Jesus Christ will come into your life and start making changes that you won't even realize are happening. He will work and mold you into what He wants you to be until the day you die. This is the reason I wrote this book: to show you that no matter what has happened in your past or what you have done, walking with Jesus Christ is the best thing that can ever happen to anyone. It is the best thing that has ever happened to me in my life. I will say that it is not going to be easy. Never ever, but it's the best thing that will ever happen to you, and the reward will be great on that day when you draw your last breath and stand before your Lord and Savior.

Reflecting on all that has happened over my life's journey, I can easily see how God had been watching over me since the day I was created by Him. Through the hardships and tears as a child, He was there. Every time I felt the deep emotional hurt and hopelessness, He was there. Throughout my fits of anger and rage, He was there. In all my years when I chose to do things my own way and be my own God, filling myself with drugs and alcohol, He was there. Sitting in that jail cell, He was there. Laying in a coma, He was there. Through seventeen surgeries, He was there. Miracle after miracle after my accident, He was there. All these trials of pain, hurt, disappointment, and destruction, and the wrong choices I made in my life, were allowed by a loving God, and they were all part of His plan to lead me *to his son*—Jesus Christ. Through it all, my heart was opened and my eyes were opened to Him. I knew His love for me and joyfully received it! God sent his only son, Jesus Christ, to pay for my sins, to die on that cross for me, a worthless sinner. It was at that point my life was changed like *water to wine* as God began to show me the awesome love and forgiveness He has for me—*and He has it for You!* Are you willing to receive it? I assure you, receiving Jesus Christ as Lord and Savior will bring you peace, joy and *abundant* life, today and forever!

One of my many favorite verses of hope is John 16:33:

"These things I have spoken to you, that in ME you may have peace. In the world you will have tribulation; but be of good cheer, I have overcome the world."

Peace and joy is ever flowing in my soul knowing Jesus Christ as my Lord and Savior, who cares for me and loves me and who I will be with in eternity after I draw my last breath! You see, death is not a bad thing when you know where you are going! Jesus will meet you wherever you are, regardless of what you have done. Today, right now, you can pray and ask to begin your changed life with Jesus. I encourage you to take a moment in the quietness, and with all sincerity in your heart, pray this simple prayer, The Sinner's Prayer:

Heavenly Father, I know I am a sinner and have done things that are wrong. I come to you in prayer asking for the forgiveness of my sins. I confess with my mouth and believe with my heart that Jesus is your son and that he died on the cross at Calvary that I might be forgiven and have eternal life with you in the Kingdom of Heaven. Father, I believe that Jesus rose from the dead, and I ask you right now to come into my life and be my personal Lord and Savior. I repent of my sins and will worship you all the days of my life! Because your word is truth, I confess with my mouth that I am born again and cleansed by the blood of Jesus! In Jesus' name, Amen.